AF599184

LET'S GET OUTDOORS!
Fishing
by Lisa Owings
BLASTOFF! 2 READERS
BELLWETHER MEDIA • MINNEAPOLIS, MN

Blastoff! Readers are carefully developed by literacy experts to build reading stamina and move students toward fluency by combining standards-based content with developmentally appropriate text.

Level 1 provides the most support through repetition of high-frequency words, light text, predictable sentence patterns, and strong visual support.

Level 2 offers early readers a bit more challenge through varied sentences, increased text load, and text-supportive special features.

Level 3 advances early-fluent readers toward fluency through increased text load, less reliance on photos, advancing concepts, longer sentences, and more complex special features.

★ **Blastoff! Universe**

Reading Level

Grade K

Grades 1–3

Grade 4

This edition first published in 2023 by Bellwether Media, Inc.

Library of Congress Cataloging-in-Publication Data

Names: Owings, Lisa, author.
Title: Fishing / by Lisa Owings.
Description: Minneapolis, MN : Bellwether Media, 2023. | Series: Blastoff! Readers : Let's get outdoors! | Includes bibliographical references and index. | Audience: Ages 5-8 | Audience: Grades 2-3 | Summary: "Relevant images match informative text in this introduction to fishing. Intended for students in kindergarten through third grade" – Provided by publisher.
Identifiers: LCCN 2022038745 (print) | LCCN 2022038746 (ebook) | ISBN 9798886871258 (library binding) | ISBN 9798886872514 (ebook)
Subjects: LCSH: Fishing–Juvenile literature.
Classification: LCC SH445 .O95 2023 (print) | LCC SH445 (ebook) | DDC 799.1–dc23/eng/20220816
LC record available at https://lccn.loc.gov/2022038745
LC ebook record available at https://lccn.loc.gov/2022038746

Editor: Rebecca Sabelko   Series Design: Andrea Schneider   Book Designer: Laura Sowers

Printed in the United States of America, North Mankato, MN.

Table of Contents

What Is Fishing?

Fishing is the activity of catching fish. **Anglers** fish in lakes, rivers, and oceans.

Some anglers fish
in **tournaments**.
Others fish just for fun!

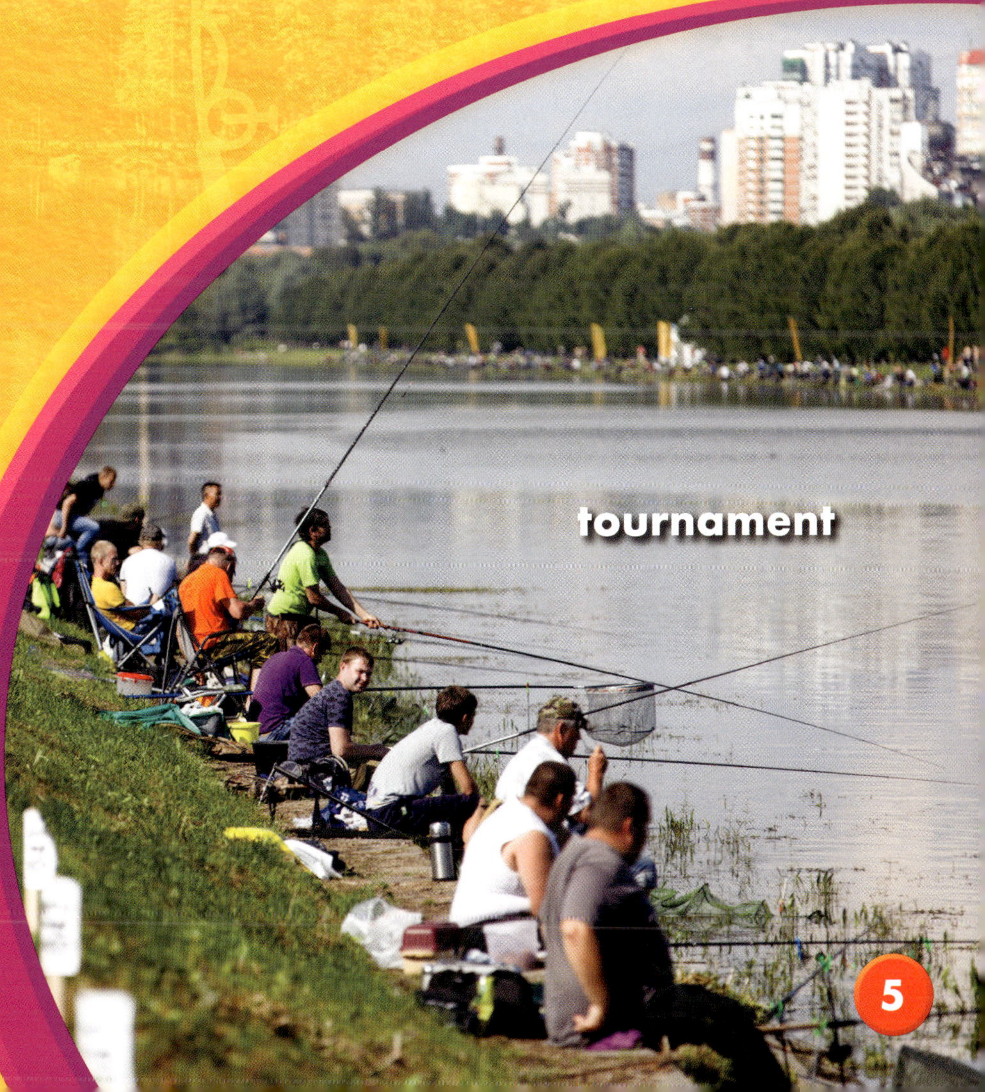

tournament

Some anglers **cast** from docks or shorelines. Others fish from boats.

Favorite Fishing Spot

Mille Lacs Lake, Minnesota

Claim to Fame

- second-largest inland lake in Minnesota
- one of the best walleye and smallmouth bass fishing lakes in the United States

Anglers can often eat the fish they catch. They can also **catch and release**.

Fish On!

Many anglers enjoy **still fishing**. Other people like fly fishing or **trolling**.

In winter, anglers go ice fishing. They drop **lines** through holes in frozen lakes or rivers.

Types of Fishing

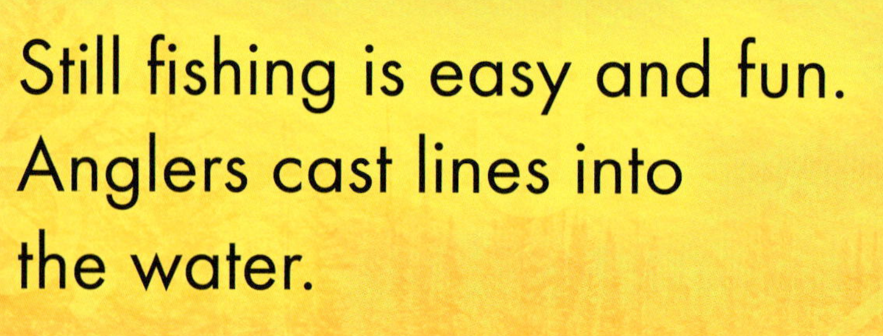

Still fishing is easy and fun. Anglers cast lines into the water.

casting

Then they wait for fish to bite.

Anglers yank their lines when they feel fish bite. Hooks poke into the fishes' mouths.

Then anglers quickly **reel** in their catches!

Fishing Gear

Anglers need a lot of gear! **Rods** and reels hold fishing lines.

Heavier rods, lines, and hooks help bring in big fish. Weights keep hooks underwater.

Anglers keep their gear in **tackle boxes**. They use **bobbers** to show when fish are biting.

Many anglers use live **bait** such as worms. Others use **lures**.

Fishing Safety

Anglers dress for the weather. They wear life jackets in boats.

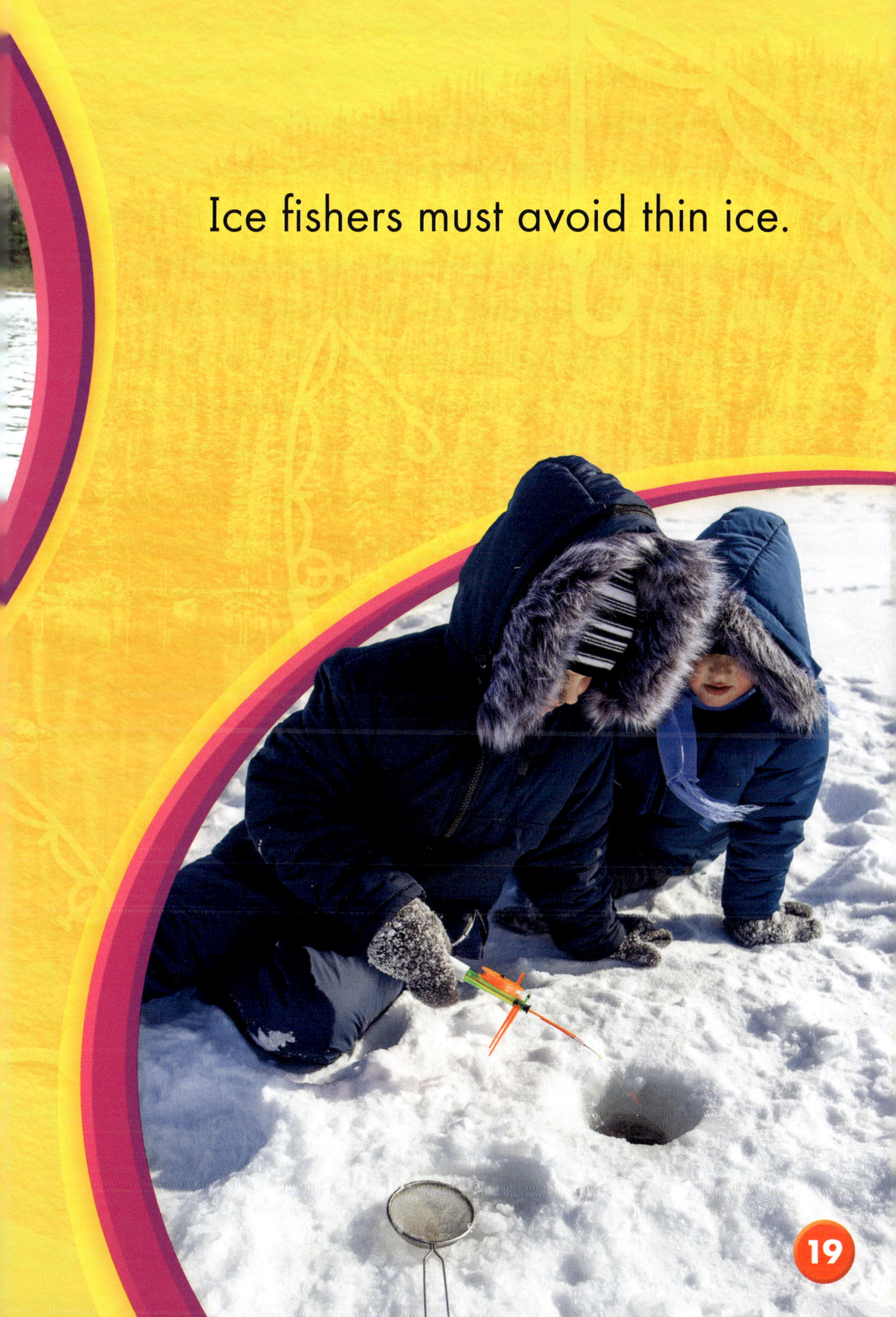

Ice fishers must avoid thin ice.

Hooks are very sharp! Anglers are careful when putting bait on hooks and removing fish.

Anglers want to land
a big one!

Glossary

anglers—people who fish with hooks and lines

bait—something used to get fish to bite a hook; bait is usually something fish eat, such as worms.

bobbers—small, floating pieces attached to fishing lines to keep hooks at certain depths; bobbers also tell anglers when fish are biting.

cast—to throw a lure or bait on a line out over the water to catch fish

catch and release—to let a fish go back into the water after it is caught

lines—long threads attached to hooks used to pull in fish

lures—fake bait; a lure looks and moves like something a fish would eat.

reel—to bring in a line by turning it around a wheel-shaped object called a reel

rods—thin, straight poles with reels and lines on them that are used for fishing

still fishing—fishing with the line and bait resting still in the water

tackle boxes—boxes that store fishing gear

tournaments—contests in which winners keep going until only one person or team is left

trolling—a type of fishing in which a line with a lure and hook is pulled through water

To Learn More

AT THE LIBRARY

Phi, Bao. *A Different Pond*. North Mankato, Minn.: Picture Window Books, 2017.

Schell, Lily. *Fantastic Fish*. Minneapolis, Minn.: Bellwether Media, 2023.

Teckentrup, Britta. *Fish Everywhere*. Somerville, Mass.: Big Picture Press, 2018.

ON THE WEB

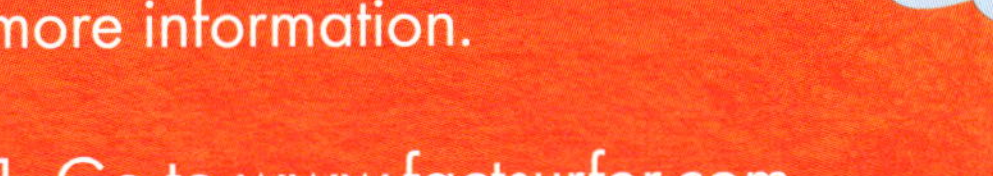

FACTSURFER

Factsurfer.com gives you a safe, fun way to find more information.

1. Go to www.factsurfer.com.
2. Enter "fishing" into the search box and click 🔍.
3. Select your book cover to see a list of related content.

Index

The images in this book are reproduced through the courtesy of: Pressmaster, front cover; gresei, p. 3; SDI Productions, pp. 4-5; Alex N, p. 5; John Brueske, p. 6; goodluz, pp. 6-7, 8-9; stockcreations, p. 7; lunamarina, pp. 8, 14-15, 23; ArtSvetlana, p. 9 (still fishing); thinair28, p. 9 (fly fishing); loveyousomuch, p. 9 (trolling); PRESSLAB, p. 9 (ice fishing); aleksander hunta, p. 10; Thomas M Perkins, pp. 10-11; redbrickstock.com/ Alamy, pp. 12-13; Afanasiev Andrii, p. 13; FedBul, p. 15; Radharc Images/ Alamy, p. 16 (tackle box); Sanit Fuangnakhon, p. 16 (fishing rod); Juhku, p. 16 (background); Joe Luis Pelaez Inc/ Getty Images, pp. 16-17; Willard, pp. 18-19; schankz, p. 19; BearFotos, p. 20; n_defender, p. 20 (hook); seanfboggs, pp. 20-21.